The Fragile Frog

by William P. Mara · illustrated by John R. Quinn

**Albert Whitman & Company,
Morton Grove, Illinois**

This book is warmly dedicated to Robert T. Zappalorti, friend and executive director of Herpetological Associates, for all he has done to preserve and protect the reptiles and amphibians of New Jersey, including the beautiful and delicate Pine Barrens treefrog, and for sharing his knowledge of this frog with me.

Thanks, too, to the many other people who gave generously of themselves for this book, especially Jerry G. Walls, who answered many detailed questions; Raymond E. Hunziker III, who discussed with me the principles of cutaneous respiration; John R. Quinn, who captures the natural world not with a net or rifle, but with pencils and brushes; Dick Bartlett, Dave Zoffer, and my dear friend Joe Collins, for all their help; my editor, Kathleen Tucker, and all the other people at Albert Whitman who worked on this book; Tracey, my wife and dearest friend, for her patience and understanding during the long nights while I did what any author must do in order to make a book worth reading; and my daughter, Lindsey Amanda, who continues to inspire me to enlighten the minds of children.

Text copyright © 1996 by William P. Mara. Illustrations copyright © 1996 by John R. Quinn.
Published in 1996 by Albert Whitman & Company, 6340 Oakton Street, Morton Grove, Illinois 60053-2723.
Published simultaneously in Canada by General Publishing, Limited, Toronto.
Printed in the United States of America.
10 9 8 7 6 5 4 3 2 1

Library of Congress Cataloging-in-Publication Data

Mara, W. P.
The fragile frog / William P. Mara; illustrated by John R. Quinn
p. cm.
Summary: Describes, in text, illustrations, and photographs, the physical characteristics, habits, and natural environment of the Pine Barrens treefrog, its endangered state, and the struggle of many frogs to survive.
ISBN 0-8075-2580-4
1. Pine Barrens treefrog—Juvenile literature. 2. Endangered species—Juvenile literature.
[1. Pine Barrens treefrog. 2. Frogs. 3. Endangered species.] I. Quinn, John R., ill. II. Title.
QL668.E24M27 1996
597.8'7—dc20   95-1409 CIP AC

Front cover photo by Animals Animals © 1996 Doug Wechsler.
Back cover photo by: Peggy A. Vargas, Nature's Images.
Designed by Scott Piehl.

Contents

A wetland in the New Jersey Pine Barrens, home of the Pine Barrens treefrog.

Introduction

The more I study frogs, the more I am fascinated by them. They are unique members of the animal world, wonderful in the way they look, in the way they live, and in the way they develop from egg to tadpole to adult.

Like all creatures, frogs have struggled to survive their natural predators and live in a constantly changing environment. Many species are hardy, adaptable, and often, just plain lucky. Other species are beginning to disappear; some are already gone. Scientists do not always know why this is happening. But more and more it is becoming evident that certain frog species are losing the battle as they struggle with changes that are a result of human behavior—as human beings, with their houses and cars and factories, spread themselves over the earth.

The Pine Barrens treefrog is just one of the fragile frogs, frogs that are not surviving harsh environmental changes and therefore are becoming endangered. Because I live in New Jersey, one of the few places where the Pine Barrens treefrog lives, I am especially fond of this frog and very aware of its fight for life.

It is my hope that as you come to know the Pine Barrens treefrog, you will gain new understanding of the problems of other frogs and all creatures, as we try to live together in our crowded world.

An adult Pine Barrens treefrog.

I.
Meet the Pine Barrens Treefrog

The Pine Barrens treefrog is one of the prettiest little animals in the world. Most of its body is green, a little lighter than the color of grass. On either side of the frog's body is a distinctive thin, dark purple or purplish-brown stripe that begins at the nose, runs around the eye and down the body, then ends near the base of the hind leg. This stripe almost always is outlined by white or very light yellow.

The frog's eyes are a rich copper color, darker than a penny. The belly is usually medium gray, like the color of the sky on an overcast day. The front legs are the same rich green as the back, but the toes are a mixture of gray and yellow or orange. The same yellow or orange color is also on the frog's hind legs, but mostly in the areas that are folded, which means the color can only be seen when the frog jumps and stretches out those legs. This type of coloration is called *flash coloring* and is used by the Pine Barrens treefrog to scare away enemies.

The female is a little larger and stouter. Some females have a white-bordered green patch on either side of the throat.

It is difficult for scientists to describe the colors of frogs and toads because they can vary so much from one individual to another within the same species.

The Amphibian Club

Like all frogs, the Pine Barrens treefrog belongs to a large group of animals known as *amphibians* (am-FIHB-ee-uhns). Amphibians include frogs and toads, which lack tails as adults; salamanders, which have long tails; and rarely seen wormlike creatures known as the *caecilians* (see-SIL-ee-uhns). Frogs and toads are called *anurans* (uh-NER-uhns), which means "tail-less." Frogs and toads are very similar, but many toads have drier, bumpier skin than frogs and can survive in drier places.

Amphibians lay "jelly"-covered eggs, with no shells, in water or moist ground. Tiny tadpoles hatch from the eggs of many amphibians and live in water until they develop into adults. Adults look very different from tadpoles and live much of the time on land.

All amphibians are *"cold-blooded,"* which means they cannot create heat within their bodies like we can (humans are *"warm-blooded"*). Instead, they must get their heat from the sun, their environment, and their behavior. When you see frogs sitting in the sunlight, they are warming their bodies in a process known as *basking*.

A Frog's Body

Frogs and toads have wide bodies and no necks. They are small creatures—very few ever grow longer than four inches, measured in their typical crouched position, from nose to rump. What is thought to be the world's largest frog, the goliath frog, is only about twelve inches long! The Pine Barrens treefrog grows no larger than two inches.

Like all adult frogs and toads, the Pine Barrens treefrog has four legs. The back legs are long and very strong, giving the frog its great leaping power. The front legs are shorter and act as shock absorbers when the frog lands.

Without any trouble at all, the Pine Barrens treefrog can leap a distance of over five feet. When you consider how tiny the frog is, that's really incredible! This talent is very useful when a frog is on the ground and wants to get back up a tree in a hurry.

With few exceptions, frogs and toads have four fingers on their hands and five toes on their feet. Some frogs have webs between their fingers and toes; these help them to be strong swimmers. On the finger and toe tips of many frogs, including the Pine Barrens treefrog, are sticky

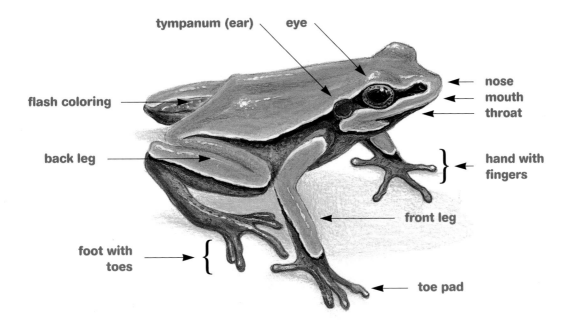

pads or disks, which act very much like suction cups. These pads help the frog hold onto leaves or branches, and they are particularly useful when the frog leaps from one spot to another to escape a predator.

Bulging from the top of either side of the Pine Barrens treefrog's rather flat head are its big eyes. Each eye has a slightly different view of the surroundings. The Pine Barrens treefrog has fairly good vision, including the ability to judge some colors and pick up very slight movement. This is important because to survive, the frog needs to catch tiny insects. Like most frogs and toads, the Pine Barrens treefrog can see at night, when it does most of its hunting. This frog has two sets of eyelids. Its opaque lids are like human eyelids and close when the animal is sleeping. The second pair of eyelids are called *nictitating* (NIHK-tih-TAY-tihng) membranes. These are translucent and act like goggles, protecting the frog's eyes when it is swimming or leaping. Most frogs have nictitating membranes.

A frog's ears are interesting. Frogs do not have outer ears, like humans. They do have eardrums, or *tympanums* (TIM-puh-nuhms). These look like little circles and can be found a short distance behind each eye. Sound travels from the tympanum through a bony middle section to the inner ear. The inner ear is connected by a nerve to the animal's brain, where sound is interpreted. Frogs and toads also pick up sounds through their front legs. A muscle structure connects the front legs directly to the inner ear. Thus, the front legs act like a pair of microphones. A Pine Barrens treefrog actually can "hear" an animal coming close to it by feeling vibrations through its front legs.

The mouth of the Pine Barrens treefrog is very wide, with small rows of teeth on the upper jaw but none on the lower. On the floor of the mouth, at the front, is a short, round, sticky tongue. Some frogs and toads have long tongues that can be fired like a slingshot to catch food. The tongue of the Pine Barrens treefrog cannot be used this way. This frog can snatch an insect only if the insect wanders very close by. Or, the frog will sneak up on the insect, grab it, and suck it up. The victim is then swallowed whole. The Pine Barrens treefrog, like most frogs, eats a great variety of insects. If a bug is small enough to fit in its mouth and unlucky enough to be quite close by, it is very likely to be eaten.

Let's Talk

Most frogs and toads have voices and can communicate with each other. The male frogs usually do most of the "talking," during breeding season. But females talk occasionally, particularly when they are alarmed or want to answer a calling male.

A frog or toad calls by taking in a deep breath, closing its mouth and nostrils, and forcing the air forward. The air then vibrates the animal's vocal cords, located in the base of its *larynx* (LAR-ihngks), at the top of its throat, in much the same way a guitar string is vibrated. Before it is exhaled through the nose or mouth, the forced air collects in an inflatable sac usually located on the animal's throat, but sometimes on either side of the neck. This sac is often called the "throat pouch."

Here's a list of what a Pine Barrens treefrog, living in New Jersey, might eat:
sow bugs
centipedes
wolf spiders
earthworms
springtails
damselflies
mayflies
dragonflies
grasshoppers
katydids
crickets
termites
cicadas
leafhoppers
beetles
moths
inchworms
caddisfly larvae
mosquitoes
bluebottle flies
houseflies
ants
daddy-longlegs

If you ever see a calling frog or toad, you will notice that the throat pouch looks like a gum bubble being blown out, then sucked back in.

Photo by: Robert T. Zappalorti, Nature's Images

A male Pine Barrens treefrog calls for a mate.

Each frog and toad species has its own unique call, and members of that species know how to recognize the call of their group and ignore the calls of others. When five or six different species are gathered at the same breeding area, they know who's who!

The call of the Pine Barrens treefrog sounds something like "quonk-quonk-quonk." You can make the sound yourself if you hold your nose and say the words slowly. Many scientists do this when they are studying Pine Barrens treefrogs in the wild and want them to come out of their hiding places.

Not Your Ordinary Skin

The skin of frogs and toads acts not only as the outside covering for the body but also as part of a frog or toad's breathing or *respiratory* system. Frogs can get a significant amount of their oxygen this way. Most active frogs cannot stay underwater for too long; they need to come to the surface and breathe through their lungs. But during the winter, when a pond may be frozen over for months, a frog hibernating underwater can get all the oxygen it needs through its skin.

This process of "breathing through the skin" is called *cutaneous* (kyu-TAY-nee-uhs) respiration. Here's how it works. Oxygen molecules in the water or air pass through the frog or toad's skin and are immediately picked up by other molecules in the blood called *hemoglobin* (HEE-moe-GLOE-bin). The hemoglobin then carries the oxygen through tiny blood vessels, or *capillaries* (KAP-uh-LEHR-ees), dispersing them throughout the animal's body. In turn, carbon dioxide molecules, which are the waste matter of many biological processes, are brought back to the skin surface and released into the air.

A frog doesn't drink through its mouth but instead absorbs water through its porous skin. If it is in dry air for too long, it may lose this water and dry up. Of course, some frogs and toads don't need as much moisture as others; their bodies have adapted to drier habitats. But all must have access to some moisture.

Scientists have learned that some toads have the ability to "taste" water through their skin. They can thus "drink" only clean, fresh water and avoid excessively salty water.

In the top photo, a Pine Barrens treefrog matches bright green moss.
In the bottom photo, the frog is darker, matching the bark of a tree.

The Pine Barrens treefrog could not survive in an arid environment like a desert. At night, when it is hunting, it absorbs moisture from the cool night air. If the weather is hot, it sits in a pond to take in water through its skin. And like all frogs, it needs moisture for breeding. Without water close by, the Pine Barrens treefrog will die.

The color of a frog's skin is very important to its survival. Many frogs and toads have skin that is the color of grass or leaves or bark, so they blend in well with their environment and avoid being seen by predators. Their natural colors provide them with camouflage (KAM-uh-FLAHZH). And the skin of frogs and toads can change color. The skin of the Pine Barrens treefrog can change from its normal medium-green color to a darker green or even to some shades of gray and brown. Sometimes this provides the frog with more protection.

There are thousands of color-containing cells called *chromatophores* (kruh-MAT-uh-fawrs) just below a frog's skin. When the light, temperature, or humidity changes, certain chromatophores grow larger while others grow smaller. Soon we can see the color of the larger chromatophores.

Can you imagine being able to peel off your outer skin when it gets old? Frogs and toads do this, the Pine Barrens treefrog included. The skin peels off fairly easily—it's a lot like pulling a sweater over your head—but unlike snakes, who leave their old skin behind once they've removed it, frogs and toads usually eat theirs.

Some toads have specialized areas of skin on the rump (called a "seat patch") and belly. These permit the toads to draw water from damp sand.

A frog pulls as much of the old skin forward as possible, then holds what has been loosened in its mouth so it can pull off the rest. The skin is thought to have some nutritional value.

Shedding is a regular activity for frogs and toads, but they don't do it according to any kind of set schedule. Scientists have noticed that frogs and toads that eat a lot shed more often than those that don't. Also, frogs and toads that have skin injuries, like cuts or scratches, will shed more frequently.

Scientists are studying secretions from the skin glands of frogs and toads to see if these powerful chemicals have medicinal value.

While normally thought of as defenseless, frogs and toads possess special skin glands that release chemical compounds as protection from predators. Depending on which species you're dealing with, these can be totally harmless, slightly irritating (the secretions may make your hands itch or your eyes burn), or deadly poisonous. Certain animals seem immune to most frog and toad poisons. Other animals can get very sick and even die if they eat a poisonous frog or a toad. Very poisonous frogs are often brightly colored, and their bright colors ward off predators.

The Pine Barrens treefrog is only mildly poisonous to some smaller animals. If you were to handle a Pine Barrens treefrog and then touch your eyes, they would be irritated. But this frog poses no serious threat to humans—though I certainly wouldn't advise eating one!

Photo by: Peggy A. Vargas, Nature's Images

The Pine Barrens treefrog was first described by a scientist in 1854, in South Carolina.

The Pine Barrens treefrog needs the trees and acidic water found in pine barrens wetlands.

Where Frogs Live

Frogs and toads can be found all over the world, in the hot rain forests near the equator and on the cold tundra of northern Canada. Most live in tropical and subtropical places. Scientists think there are more than thirty-eight hundred *species*, or different kinds. Frogs occupy many types of *habitats*. A habitat is an animal's natural environment— the particular temperature, soil, water, vegetation, and other animal life that allow it to live and thrive.

The Pine Barrens treefrog lives only in the United States, and only in five states—New Jersey, North Carolina, South Carolina, Florida, and Alabama.

True to its name, this frog is found most often in pine barrens—quiet wooded areas made up mostly of pine trees and dry, sandy soil. But don't let this general description mislead you. There can be many other, more specialized habitats found within a pine barrens, including some very wet areas, such as shrub bogs and cedar swamps. These watery places are home to the Pine Barrens treefrog. They are *wetlands*.

There may be many species of frogs that haven't even been discovered yet. Most of these are thought to live in rain forests.

A wetland is land that is almost always wet because it lies so close to its water source. A wetland area contains bodies of water that are either very slow moving or not moving at all. Wetlands help regulate the water cycle, filter water, and prevent soil erosion. A wetland is also home to many creatures; scientists have determined that one-third of all the endangered species in the United States breed in wetland areas.

The water in the habitat of the Pine Barrens treefrog is very acidic. Scientists have found that this acid water is necessary for the eggs of the Pine Barrens treefrog to develop.

In their wetland habitats, Pine Barrens treefrogs spend their days resting on the branches of bushes and small trees, crawling to the ground at night to hunt or to gather around breeding pools in the spring. Because they spend so much time in trees, they are called *arboreal* (are-BORE-ee-uhl) animals.

It is thought that some frogs developed into arboreal animals because, millions of years ago, life became too competitive for them. There were too many other creatures living on the ground that were better at catching food or, even worse, catching *them* for food. Pine Barrens treefrogs, along with many other treefrog species, survived by adapting to life in the trees.

Hibernation

During the colder parts of the year, the Pine Barrens treefrog goes through a period of *hibernation*. During this time all of its metabolic functions, including heart rate, breathing, and brain activity, slow almost to a full stop. Because Pine Barrens treefrogs are cold-blooded animals, low winter temperatures force them into hibernation (unlike hibernating bears, for example, that are warm-blooded and therefore can be active during the winter).

A hibernating Pine Barrens treefrog will not eat or drink, and it barely even moves. It hibernates underground a short distance below the frost level, perhaps in a gopher burrow or a network of tree roots. It can also hibernate underwater in a cedar swamp. Even Pine Barrens treefrogs that live in areas where the winters are very mild, like Florida, still go through a brief "cooling" period in which their bodies shut down for a short time. However, hibernation for them certainly isn't as long as it is for their relatives in the north.

At the Breeding Pool

In the spring, the Pine Barrens treefrogs emerge from hibernation and begin gathering around what are called *breeding pools*. These pools are created when the spring rains fill up the many shallow depressions found in their habitat. The frogs often use the same pools year after year.

At the breeding pools, the males begin calling for mates, usually during or just after heavy rainstorms and almost always at night. If a male's call is appealing enough, a female will approach him. The male then jumps on her back, and the two of them leap together into the water. The joined-together position they are in during this breeding time is called *amplexus* (am-PLEX-us).

The female Pine Barrens treefrog releases her eggs into the water—as many as eight hundred!—while the male fertilizes them with his sperm. Many frogs and toads release their eggs in long, stringy tubes, but the Pine Barrens treefrog releases eggs one at a time. This improves each egg's chance of survival. If a hungry bird or snake comes into one of the breeding pools and finds a large pile of frog

Photo by: Saul Friess, Nature's Images

The male frog tightly grips the female, then releases sperm into the water as she releases eggs.

eggs, it will eat them all. If the eggs have drifted all over the breeding pool, the predator may find only a few, and the rest will have a chance to develop into tadpoles.

Once the eggs are fertilized, they sink to the bottom of the pool or stick to the stems and leaves of underwater plants. Each one is covered with a sticky, jellylike goo that helps keep them firmly in place while the embryo develops. Depending on how warm the water is, it will take from a few days to almost two weeks for the eggs to hatch.

Like adult frogs, many tadpoles change color in reaction to light.

Once the embryo has completed its development in the egg capsule, out comes the tadpole! This little creature can be a range of colors, from pale yellow to olive, and is covered with dark spots. It is smaller than a dime and shaped like a jellybean with a tailfin. Once hatched, the "tad" of the Pine Barrens treefrog begins one of the most fascinating and miraculous processes in the animal world—*metamorphosis* (MEHT-uh-MAWR-fuh-sihs)—the change in form from one life stage to the next.

Metamorphosis

For the first twenty-four hours, the Pine Barrens tadpole has rows of *gill stalks* on either side of its head. Each stalk looks like a feathery vine. The stalks help the tadpole breathe by processing oxygen molecules from the water since the animal doesn't have any lungs yet. Towards the end of this twenty-four-hour period, the gill stalks draw back into the tadpole's body, leaving only their tips peeking out from inside the *gills*. The tadpole will continue to breathe by absorbing oxygen from water flowing into its gills.

Recently scientists have discovered that some tadpoles can recognize their siblings and cousins!

During the next five to seven weeks, the tadpole eats and grows, using its tiny rows of teeth to nibble on the plant matter and algae in its birthing pool. It slowly becomes darker in color. It is during this stage of life that the tadpole is in the greatest peril, for it is almost totally helpless against creatures that might want to eat it. Although it can sense trouble, it can only swim away a short distance and hide in the plant gardens of its watery home.

As with the young of all frogs and toads, most will not survive. During its lifetime, a female Pine Barrens treefrog could lay three thousand to six thousand eggs, but less than 5 percent will survive to become mature adults, capable of producing more frogs.

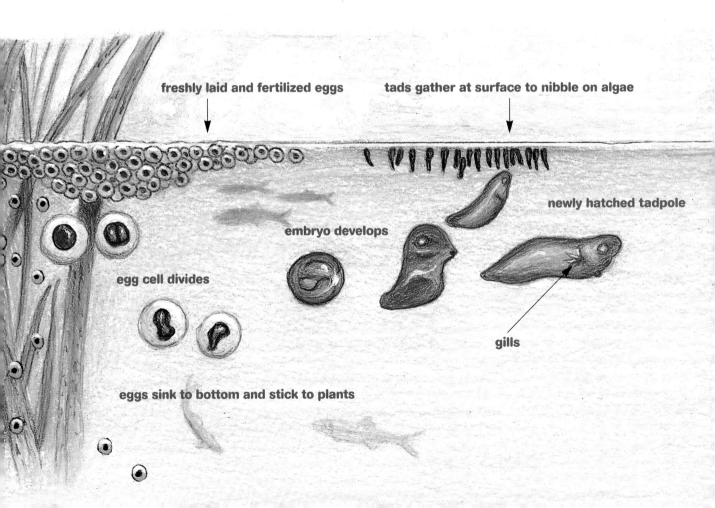

freshly laid and fertilized eggs

tads gather at surface to nibble on algae

newly hatched tadpole

embryo develops

egg cell divides

gills

eggs sink to bottom and stick to plants

If the tadpole lives until its sixth or seventh week, its legs begin to appear and the tail starts to shrink. (It is eventually absorbed into the frog's body.) The hind legs come first, appearing as little bumps at the front of the tailfin until they finally develop into hind legs. The front legs develop inside the gills and emerge shortly before metamorphosis is completed.

During the last five to ten days, major physical changes will take place in the frog's mouth parts and digestive organs as it changes from a plant-eating tadpole to a meat-eating adult. Until these changes are complete, the frog does not eat and draws upon fat, mostly stored in its tail, to meet its energy needs. The eyes, which were formerly on either side of the tadpole's head, move a little closer to the top of the head. The tympanum and the rest of the ear structure develop. The

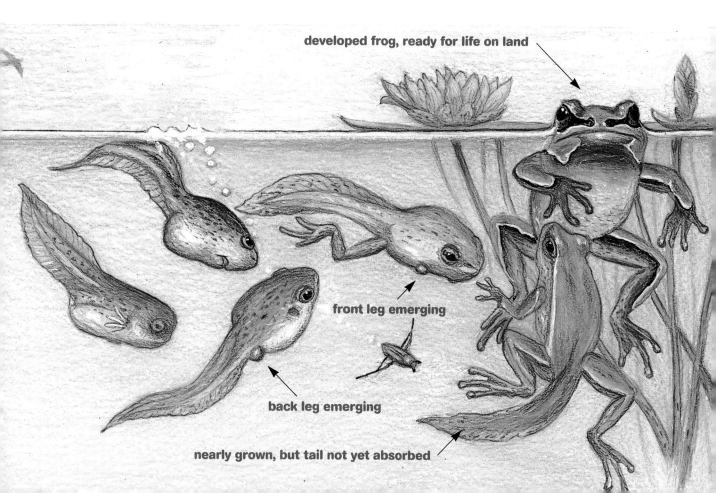

developed frog, ready for life on land

front leg emerging

back leg emerging

nearly grown, but tail not yet absorbed

mouth becomes larger and moves forward. The lungs form, and as they do, a connection between them and the tadpole's nose and mouth develops. Because of this, the tad no longer will breathe through its gills but instead through its nose and mouth and skin.

As its breathing system matures, the young frog will spend a lot of time between water and land, shifting back and forth from gill-breathing to nose-and-mouth breathing. Now there are new dangers. If the breeding pool dries up before the the frog can use its lungs, it may die. Likewise, if the frog can't find land when its lungs are ready for air, it cannot survive.

In the last week of metamorphosis, the now land-dwelling Pine Barrens treefrog will hang around the shoreline of its breeding pool and eat its first meal made up of animal rather than plant matter. It cannot eat anything very large; small spiders and very tiny insects such as springtails and newly hatched crickets are favored foods of very hungry young Pine Barrens treefrogs.

Shortly thereafter, the young frog will take to the bushes and trees and begin its life on land. Two to three years will have to pass before the animal is old enough to produce its own young. The normal lifespan of the Pine Barrens treefrog is five to seven years.

2.
The Fight for Survival

Pine Barrens treefrogs are rare. In fact, there are so few of them they are considered an endangered species in all five of their native states. This means it is very possible that soon there will be no Pine Barrens treefrogs at all—every single one will be gone. The species that was the Pine Barrens treefrog will be wiped from the earth, forever.

To find out how many Pine Barrens treefrogs are around, scientists go into their habitats and locate groups of frogs, called *populations* or *colonies*. They determine how many colonies are in a particular area; then they try to count how many individuals make up a particular colony. Of course, it's hard to know if all the frogs have come forward to be counted! Still, it's possible to get a good idea of how many animals are living in a given year.

Studies that began in New Jersey in 1959 and continued for about twenty years showed that the number of colonies was lowering dramatically. By 1987, colonies in some places had entirely disappeared. In other habitats, the number of colonies was greatly reduced. So what exactly has been happening to the Pine Barrens treefrog? Scientists think they have some answers.

To find the tiny Pine Barrens treefrog, scientists must sometimes wade through wetland habitats in the dark, searching with flashlights and imitating the mating call.

I'm Hungry, You're Hungry

Like all animals, the Pine Barrens treefrog is always struggling to survive. Some of its battle is against the natural world and its processes.

Frogs are an important part of the food chain. Many animals see frogs as only one thing—dinner. For example, when a large garter snake gets hungry, it crawls towards a nearby pond to search for a meal. Garter snakes have a very varied diet and will eat many animals, including small fish, salamanders, newts, other snakes, worms, slugs, crayfish, and frogs. Scientists have learned that garter snakes living in the same areas as Pine Barrens treefrogs include them in their diet, and the snakes eat not only the adult frogs but the tadpoles as well.

Garter snakes aren't the only animals that prey on the Pine Barrens treefrog. Other kinds of snakes, beetles, newts, and turtles go to frog breeding pools in search of frogs and tadpoles. Some leeches and fish feed on the eggs of the Pine Barrens treefrog.

Of course, the Pine Barrens treefrog must eat, too. Its diet consists largely of spiders and insects such as crickets, beetles, and flies. But the Pine Barrens treefrog is not the only animal in its habitat that eats these creatures. They make up an important part of the diet of salamanders, fish, snakes, birds, and small mammals.

The Pine Barrens treefrog is not a very aggressive hunter. It may leap after very small prey if it is particularly hungry, but mostly it just sits and waits for insects to fly by. In some years, when the competition for food is very intense, many Pine Barrens treefrogs starve to death.

The Changing Environment

All creatures are affected by the environment, which is constantly changing. In a process called *natural succession*, all of the characteristics of a particular environment go through changes over the course of time. Since everything in an environment is delicately balanced, when one small change occurs, everything else changes as well. Usually these changes are very minor—the water level in a pond rises because the volume of rainfall is greater in a particular year, for example. But other times changes can be sudden and violent, caused by earthquakes, severe flooding, drought, volcanic eruptions, and major storms like hurricanes and tornadoes.

Natural succession affects the life of the Pine Barrens treefrog. If one year the winter season lasts a little longer than usual, the spring rains will be late. Then, if warm weather comes on schedule, the breeding pools will dry up too soon for the developing tadpoles to reach the point where they can live on land.

If a certain plant suddenly begins to thrive, it may crowd out another kind of plant. If the plant that dies is the only food source for a particular type of insect, the insect will not survive in that habitat. And if that insect was a main food source for Pine Barrens treefrogs, many of the frogs will die of starvation.

In the pine barrens environment, the cattail is often an *invader plant*— a plant that takes over once it gets established. The cattail is a tall and slender-leafed plant with a flower that looks like a velvety brown stalk. It produces thousands of little seeds. When a strong wind blows, these

lightweight seeds detach and can be carried great distances. The seeds easily root themselves along shores of ponds in the wetland habitats of Pine Barrens treefrogs. Cattails grow very quickly. Once they have established themselves, they crowd other plants, causing them to die out. Now the balance of the insect life may be thrown off. The cattails can also absorb rainwater, preventing it from running into a pond and thereby causing the pond to dry up more quickly than usual.

Some animals have the ability to adjust to environmental changes; these are considered more *adaptable* animals. Adaptable animals will survive in an environment that has been altered, or they have the means to find another location that is right for them.

Garter snakes are highly adaptable. Because they eat many kinds of food and are very hardy, they don't need to live in a particular area. If all the earthworms in their habitat die, they will eat the crickets and slugs instead. If the water dries up in their pond, some will travel as far as a mile to find another food-rich pond area.

Water snakes also travel from one habitat to another when they need to. When this happens, Pine Barrens treefrogs can be affected. If there is an unusually great amount of rain one year, a lake or pond may overflow, and the excess water may spill over into the breeding pond of a Pine Barrens treefrog. Small fish may also spill into the pool, attracting water snakes. While hunting for food, the hungry water snakes will notice the frogs, and soon the frogs will become their prey as well.

Other animals are more *specialized*. They have very strict requirements and cannot adjust to many changes in their environment. The Pine Barrens treefrog is considered a specialized animal. It must live in an area that has plenty of shrubs and trees. It must stay near a permanent water source. It eats only very small insects that are close by. And although this frog can leap five feet, it usually doesn't travel far, preferring to stay in a relatively small area, or *home range*. The Pine Barrens treefrog is simply not very well equipped to change its lifestyle.

It is important to note that not all frogs and toads are as specialized as the Pine Barrens treefrog. Some are as adaptable as garter snakes, which is why frogs and toads as a group have survived as long as they have. Even the harshest of natural changes have not wiped out these amphibians.

But the Pine Barrens treefrog, along with other frogs and toads, is now beginning to seriously feel the effect of a more dangerous threat—the human race.

Destroying Frogs' Homes

Humans have destroyed many of the natural places where animals live. Every time a few hundred acres of forest, wetlands, or prairie are bull-dozed to build houses, office buildings, or parking lots, the homes of all the creatures that live there disappear.

About 65 million years ago, cataclysmic changes in the environment caused many animal species, including dinosaurs, to become extinct. Frogs, however, continued to survive. Can they continue to adapt to life with human beings?

Photo by: Peggy A. Vargas, Nature's Images

A habitat is destroyed for construction.

Ever since World War II, a great deal of construction has been going on in many places where Pine Barrens treefrogs live. Often a wetland area is drained before homes or roads are built. This destroys the home of many frogs. Every time a natural pool is drained or filled in with topsoil or cement, another population of frogs dies.

31

The habitat of the Pine Barrens treefrog can also be damaged if too much water is added. This usually happens when a temporary pool is deepened so it can become a large pond, stocked with fish for food or sport. Now the fish will eat whatever happens to be in the water, including tadpoles. Because the pool is deeper it will not dry up like it used to; this means that most, if not all, of the tadpoles will drown because they will not be able to reach land at the critical point in their development where they must begin to use their lungs for breathing.

People often damage habitats without even realizing it. When trucks or motorcycles are driven through the Pine Barrens treefrogs' breeding pools, not only does the delicate plant and insect life of the pool become upset, but many tadpoles and frogs get crushed and killed. Or sometimes the tads are thrown from the water and cannot get back into it.

When people cut down trees and bushes to clear land for building or just for firewood, the Pine Barren treefrogs' habitat is badly affected, for the frogs cannot survive on the ground.

Pollution

The effects of pollution on the air, water, and soil have been devastating. Delicate habitats have been irreparably damaged, and entire animal populations have been wiped out.

For example, the lesser siren, an aquatic salamander found primarily in the southeastern United States, was eradicated from some parts of

Louisiana when hundreds of gallons of chemicals were dumped into the lakes and ponds where this amphibian lived. These chemicals were intended to kill off certain species of fish in order to make room for game fish. But the chemicals killed off not only fish and the lesser siren salamander populations, but many bullfrog, leopard frog, and green frog populations as well.

Scientists believe that pollution is also the main reason for the disappearance of many populations of the tiny and very beautiful cricket frog all over the eastern United States.

The Pine Barrens treefrog has been affected by pollution, too. It has been especially damaged by *road runoff*. Road runoff results when rainwater mixes with the gasoline, oil, and petroleum hydrocarbons (the gases that leak and blow out of a car's exhaust pipe) that cover roads. This contaminated water runs off the roads and into the wetlands. In the same way that a sponge absorbs water, the wetland environment absorbs the runoff, and the Pine Barrens treefrogs' habitat becomes poisonous. Because a frog's skin is so porous, chemicals can very quickly penetrate its system. It is only a short time before the frogs, both newborn and adult, begin to die.

Chemical materials used in farming also affect the Pine Barrens treefrog. Pesticides (used for killing organisms harmful to crops) and fertilizers (which help crops grow bigger and faster) can be absorbed into an environment, just like road runoff. And like road runoff, farming chemicals will poison the water in the habitat, eventually killing the frogs. Chemicals can also upset the acidic balance of the breeding pools, so that the eggs do not develop.

Ozone Damage

Ozone is a form of oxygen. It is found in the stratosphere, one of the layers of gases surrounding the earth. There, ozone filters out harmful rays given off by the sun, most particularly ultraviolet rays. Ultraviolet rays are very powerful, and while they benefit life in some ways (they stimulate bone growth in mammals and hormones needed for breeding), they also encourage the development of skin cancer and can slowly cause blindness in mammals, including human beings.

Scientists have come to the conclusion that the ozone layer is weakening. This weakness is thought to be caused by the pollution of chemical compounds called *chlorofluorocarbons* (KLAWR-oh-FLUR-oh-KAHR-buhns), often referred to as fluorocarbons or "CFCs."

CFCs were originally developed to replace highly toxic and flammable substances used in refrigerators and air conditioners. They also have been used in aerosol cans and as cleansing agents for electronic equipment. CFCs have been released into the air all over the world.

In the mid-1970s, scientists at the University of California at Irvine identified CFCs as the main cause of ozone-layer destruction. CFCs float up into the ozone layer where ultraviolet light strikes them, releasing chlorine. The chlorine destroys ozone molecules, thus creating holes and weaknesses in the ozone layer. Many countries, including the United States, are working to stop the release of CFCs into the atmosphere. But because CFCs have a long lifespan, they will float in the air for many years, further weakening the ozone layer and allowing more ultraviolet rays to reach us.

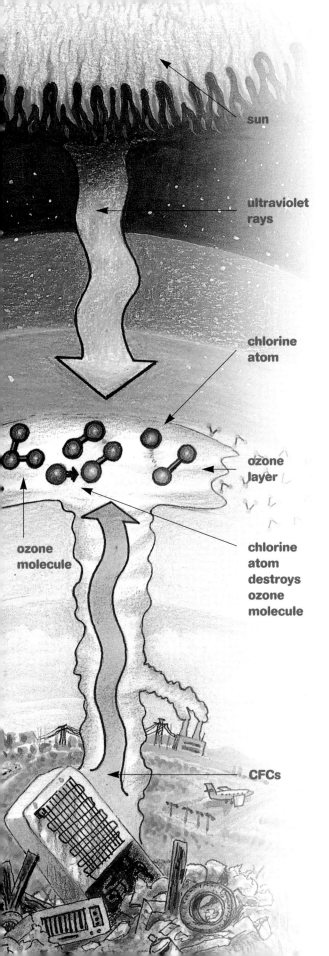

sun

ultraviolet
rays

chlorine
atom

ozone
layer

chlorine
atom
destroys
ozone
molecule

ozone
molecule

CFCs

Scientists believe the increased amount of ultraviolet light can destroy the eggs of many amphibians species. Those that have suffered most live in the mountains, in high-elevation regions, where the ultraviolet rays are strongest. But in any region, breeding ponds that are not shaded by tall plants or leafy overhanging tree branches have the potential to become death traps for delicate eggs because they are more exposed to ultraviolet rays.

In 1993 and 1994, a team of scientists led by Dr. Andrew Blaustein of Oregon State University conducted experiments on the eggs of frogs, toads, and salamanders in the Cascade Mountains of Oregon. A portion of a pond containing eggs was shaded with a piece of plastic that filtered out ultraviolet radiation. The rest of the pond remained unshaded.

The scientists discovered that more than 90 percent of the salamander eggs in the unshaded area did not hatch. Only 45 percent of those in the shaded area failed to hatch. Of the frog and toad eggs, about 40 percent of those that were unshaded perished, while only 10 to 20 percent of the protected eggs didn't make it.

The eggs of one particular frog species, the Pacific treefrog, did not suffer to any great extent. The scientists soon figured out

Tadpoles in a breeding pool.

why. These eggs contained an unusually high amount of something called *photolyase* (FOH-toh-layz), an enzyme that protects the eggs from ultraviolet radiation.

Dr. Blaustein concluded that ultraviolet radiation plays a large role in the dying-off of some amphibian species. While scientists do not believe the ozone problem has as yet been harmful to the Pine Barrens treefrog, this frog's eggs could easily become damaged in unshaded breeding pools if the ozone layer continues to be weakened.

Frogs As Pets

Any animal that is not protected by federal or state law can be taken from its wild home, put in a bag or cage, and brought to a pet store where it will be sold and then kept captive for the rest of its life.

Until the 1970s the Pine Barrens treefrog was one of these unprotected animals. Because the frogs are so pretty, many people wanted to have them for pets. For years, thousands were taken from their woodland homes and sold. They rarely lived long in captivity, but still the demand for them remained steady.

After people had collected the Pine Barrens treefrog for years, the populations were greatly reduced. Every time a collector took a male frog from the wild, there was one less male to breed with a female. Every time a female was taken, there was one less female to produce thousands of eggs.

What saved the Pine Barrens treefrogs, and many other animals, was a series of protection laws passed in the late 1970s by the United States government and state governments. These laws stated that anyone taking endangered species from the wild would suffer severe penalties, including heavy fines and possibly time in jail. The laws worked— many endangered species, including the Pine Barrens treefrog, disappeared from the pet trade and are now virtually never seen in captivity, except in zoos and academic institutions.

3.
More Fragile Frogs

In 1989, the First World Congress of Herpetology was held in Canterbury, England. There, herpetologists (scientists who study reptiles and amphibians) began to talk about the disappearance of frogs and toads.

All over the world, frogs and toads have been disappearing. The golden toad, found near Monteverde, Costa Rica, hasn't been seen since 1989. In Australia, the gastric brooding frog, an unusual species whose babies develop in the female's stomach, was discovered in 1974 but disappeared six years later. The California red-legged frog is endangered, as are many frogs and toads in that state.

Why is this happening? Scientists have some answers. Certainly, habitat destruction is a major reason. When forests are cut down, when wetlands are drained or filled to construct roads or buildings, habitats are destroyed, and frogs cannot survive. The damaged ozone layer appears to be a serious problem for some species. Trouble may be caused by global warming, which can affect the amount of moisture in the ground. And acid rain (rain that has mixed with gases created by the burning of fuels such as coal and oil) can harm eggs and tadpoles when it soaks into breeding pools. Widespread use of pesticides, especially DDT, for agriculture and mosquito control undoubtedly has resulted in the killing of many frog and toad populations.

Other frog species are almost extinct because people have collected them for food—some people consider frog legs a gourmet treat.

Probably in many cases there is no single reason—a frog population may decline because of disease, weather, pollution and other human activity, natural succession, and other factors that are still unknown.

Here are some more frog stories.

The Wyoming Toad

The Wyoming toad is found only in the state of Wyoming. Like other toads, it is short, stout, and covered with warts. Its basic color is brown, greenish-brown, or light gray. A thin, light-colored (usually off-white) stripe runs down the middle of its back. The belly is usually white with a collection of light gray spots. The toad's sides are light yellow.

Most toads are only fair swimmers, but Wyoming toads are at home in the water. They usually stay close to ponds and streams and will dive into the water when they sense danger. They do most of their hunting during the day, but they may come out on very warm summer nights as well. The males have a beautiful call that sounds like a soft trill.

As far as scientists knew, Wyoming toads lived only in a small habitat near Laramie. Over the last few decades, their home has been sprayed with aerial pesticides and contaminated with pollution from pasture runoff. Breeding pools have dried up because river water was diverted to another area. By 1983, scientists couldn't find even a single specimen, and the Wyoming toad was considered lost.

 Then, in 1987, a fisherman discovered a group of them in Mortenson Lake, about ten miles west of Laramie. But that colony found itself in serious trouble very quickly; in a few years its population was drastically reduced. In 1991, only three females bred. This breeding occurred in muddy tire ruts and two shallow depressions that had been made the previous winter by boats stored on the lakeside marsh. The tadpoles were in immediate danger from lack of water. There had been a drought the year before, and the water level of the lake was lowered. To save the tads, the Wyoming Fish and Game Department, together with the U.S. Fish and Wildlife Service, had to pump water back into the tadpoles' pools.

In 1992, no breedings at all occurred at Mortenson Lake, and a captive-breeding program was begun. The captive-bred tadpoles were introduced back into the habitat at Mortenson Lake and into another nearby site, Lake George. (Much of the toad habitat around Mortenson Lake was purchased by a conservation group.) Since the program began, no Wyoming toads have bred naturally at Mortenson Lake, but more tadpoles have begun appearing at Lake George. It is possible that the Laramie habitat has become too altered for the Wyoming toad to live there. Scientists hope that the toads will survive at the Lake George site, but this species will continue to walk the fine line between existence and extinction until its numbers become much larger.

The Western Toad

Western toads live in western North America, mostly along the Pacific coast from southern Alaska to Baja California, Mexico, and as far east as western and central Alberta, Canada, as well as the states of Montana, Wyoming, Utah, Colorado, and Nevada. They can be found in a variety of habitats, including mountain meadows, grasslands, woodlands, and desert streams and springs. They are usually light tan, gray, brown, or greenish-gray in color, and their warts, which are sometimes tinged rusty-red, are set into black blotches.

These toads eat just about anything they can fit into their mouths, and they breed in great numbers every year. They seemed like one group that would never disappear.

Then in the early 1970s, scientists who were studying western toads were horrified to discover that the populations were shrinking rapidly. One year a hundred specimens would be counted at a particular site; the next year only five. The year after that, there would be no toads at all. Soon, more than 75 percent of the toads had vanished. Many scientists believe the western toads suffered from a breakdown in their immune system. They were not able to fight off infections they normally should have been able to resist. In particular, they contracted "redleg" disease, so called because it brings on massive hemorrhaging, or bleeding, and the blood is brought to the surface of the skin, especially on the legs.

Even scientists who have studied the western toads' tragedy for years still do not know what has caused it. Luckily, at least for now, there are enough toads to keep the species alive.

The Cascades Frog

The Cascade and Olympic mountain ranges in the northwestern United States are the only places where this frog lives. It is light brown or greenish-brown, with inky black spots on its back. The undersides of its body and legs are yellow or yellowish-tan.

The Cascades frog seldom strays far from water. It can be found in or near streams, in shallow pools in wetland meadows, and along the

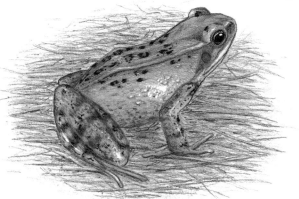

edges of ponds and lakes in quiet, mountainous areas. When it breeds, it lays its eggs in shallow water that is totally exposed to direct sunlight. This is one reason why the Cascades frog is moving closer toward extinction—its eggs are being damaged by ultraviolet rays.

The Las Vegas Leopard Frog

This handsome frog's story is the saddest, for it is already extinct.

The backs of the Las Vegas leopard frogs were green or brown, and the frogs were covered with small, dark spots. Their bellies were whitish, and the undersides of their back legs were golden yellow. They grew over three inches long, about the size of a baseball card. They could be found only near springs and seepage areas in Clark County, Nevada.

Then, in the 1920s and 1930s, the town of Las Vegas began to grow into a big city. All of the water where the Las Vegas leopard frogs lived was pumped out, and often the land was filled in with cement. Some of the frogs' breeding ponds were stocked with large and hungry game fish, which began feeding on the tadpoles.

A few scientists saw what was happening, but by the time they began to study the breeding pools, it was already too late. What was perhaps the last living specimen was seen in 1942. It was a small male, sitting on the edge of a pool in the middle of the night, calling for a mate.

His call would go forever unanswered.

Can the Frogs Be Saved?

Some people find it hard to understand why we should worry about saving frogs from extinction. Frogs do not seem very impressive. They aren't powerful, like eagles or whales, and they don't look soft and lovable, like pandas.

But all creatures in the natural world are valuable. Each is an important link in the chain of life; each is beautiful and fascinating and in some way provides unique information about all living beings, including ourselves.

Many scientists believe that because some frogs are so fragile, they are especially affected by environmental problems. Their troubles are a warning about what could happen to other animals, including human beings, if pollution problems become worse, if the ozone layer is more damaged, if more forests are cut down, if more pesticides are used.

Since the late 1980s, scientists have been working to figure out why frogs are disappearing. They have been searching in frog habitats all over the world to count populations and look for missing species. They have held meetings, conducted experiments, written articles, and worked to get money so they can do more research. They have tried to get people to pay attention to the problems of frogs and toads. Captive-breeding programs have been developed for some frog and toad species whose habitats have been so abused that there is no place for them to live on earth.

Just learning about frogs is a very important step. As people have become aware of other endangered animals, some important things have happened. Governments have passed laws monitoring the collection and shipment of endangered animals, including frogs. Clean air and water regulations have been established. World leaders are working to protect the ozone layer.

There are many simple things people can do. Frogs and tadpoles should not be taken out of the woods and put in cages or jars. Campers and hikers should be very careful not to damage delicate wetland habitats. Everyone must be careful not to waste natural resources; as more paper is used, for example, more forests must be cut down to supply it.

Sometimes, the choices are difficult. The world's population is becoming larger and larger. Should a wetland be drained to provide more housing? Should a wildlife area be opened to the public so that people who live in cities can go camping? Should poor countries destroy rain forests for food or fuel?

These are not easy decisions. But we must somehow figure out a way to allow life to go on for all creatures on our planet. There is nothing *frogs* can do; it is up to us.

Photo by: Robert T. Zappalorti, Nature's Images

Bibliography

The following books and articles were helpful in writing this book. Titles preceded by an asterisk were written for young people.

Books

*Back, Christine, and Barrie, Watts. *Tadpole and Frog.* Stopwatch Series. Morristown, N.J.: Silver Burdett, 1986.

Behler, John L., and F. Wayne King. *The Audubon Society Field Guide to North American Reptiles and Amphibians.* New York: Knopf, 1979.

Boyd, Howard P. *A Field Guide to the Pine Barrens of New Jersey.* Longview, Wash.: Plexus, 1991.

*Clarke, Barry. *Amazing Frogs and Toads.* Eyewitness Juniors Series. New York: Knopf, 1991.

*Cole, Joanna. *A Frog's Body.* New York: Morrow, 1980.

Commoner, Barry. *Making Peace with the Planet.* New York: Pantheon, 1990.

Conant, Roger, and Joseph T. Collins. *A Field Guide to Reptiles and Amphibians, Eastern and Central North America.* Boston: Houghton-Mifflin, 1991.

DeGraaff, Robert M. *The Book of the Toad.* Rochester, Vt.: Park Street Press, 1991.

Forman, Richard T. T. *Pine Barrens: Ecosystem and Landscape.* San Diego: Academic Press, 1979.

*Fowler, Allan. *Frogs and Toads and Tadpoles Too.* Chicago: Childrens Press, 1992.

*Gerholdt, James E. *Treefrogs.* Amazing Amphibians Series. Minneapolis: Abdo, 1994.

*Hogan, Paula Z. *The Frog.* Life Cycles Books. Austin, Tex.: Raintree Steck-Vaughn, 1979.

*Johnson, Sylvia A. *Tree Frogs.* Lerner Natural Science Books. Minneapolis: Lerner, 1986.

McCormick, Jack. *The Pine Barrens, A Preliminary Ecological Inventory.* Trenton: New Jersey State Museum, 1970.

Moler, Paul E., ed. *Rare and Endangered Biota of Florida.* Vol. 3, *Amphibians and Reptiles.* Gainesville, Fla.: University Press of Florida, 1992.

Noble, G. Kingsley. *The Biology of the Amphibia.* Mineola, N.Y.: Dover, 1954.

*Oda, Hidetomo. *The Tadpole.* Nature Close-Ups Series. Austin, Tex.: Raintree Steck-Vaughn, 1986.

*———. *The Tree Frog.* Nature Close-Ups Series. Austin, Tex.: Raintree Steck-Vaughn, 1986.

*Parker, Steve. *Frogs and Toads.* San Francisco: Sierra Club Books for Children, 1994.

*Pfeffer, Wendy. *From Tadpole to Frog.* Let's-Read-and-Find Out Science Book: Stage One. New York: HarperCollins, 1994.

Phillips, Kathryn. *Tracking the Vanishing Frogs.* New York: St. Martin's, 1994.

*Pringle, Laurence. *Vanishing Ozone: Protecting Earth from Ultraviolet Radiation.* New York: Morrow, 1995.

*Riley, Helen. *Frogs and Toads.* Weird and Wonderful Series. New York: Thomson Learning, 1993.

Roan, Sharon L. *Ozone Crisis: The 15 Year Evolution of a Sudden Global Emergency.* New York: John Wiley, 1990.

Schneider, Stephen H. *Global Warming.* San Francisco: Sierra Club, 1989.

*Seibert, Patricia. *Toad Overload: A True Tale of Nature Knocked Off Balance in Australia.* Brookfield, Conn.: Millbrook, 1995.

Zug, George R. *Herpetology, An Introductory Biology of Amphibians and Reptiles.* San Diego: Academic Press, 1993.

Articles and Papers

Anderson, Karen, and Paul E. Moler. "Natural Hybrids of the Pine Barrens Treefrog, *Hyla andersoni,* with *H. cinerea* and *H. femoralis* (Anura, Hylidae): Morphological and Chromosomal Evidence." *Copeia* 1(1986): 70-76.

Aronson, Lester R. "The Sexual Behavior of Anura—the 'Release' Mechanism and Sex Recognition in *H. andersoni.*" *Copeia* 4 (1943): 246-49.

Bartlett, R. D. "Hot Days, Dry Nights, and Pine Barrens Treefrogs." *Vivarium* 3, no.1 (May/June 1991): 24-29.

Blair, W. Frank. "Call Structure and Species Groups in U.S. Tree Frogs *(Hyla)*." *Southwestern Naturalist* 3, nos. 1-4, 1958 (1959): 77-89.

Bullard, A. J. "Additional Records of the Treefrog *Hyla andersoni* from the Coastal Plain of North Carolina." *Herpetologica* 21, no. 2 (June 25, 1965): 154-55.

Conant, Roger. "Reptiles and Amphibians of the New Jersey Pine Barrens." *New Jersey Nature News* 17, no.1 (1962): 16-21.

————, and R. M. Bailey. "Some Herpetological Records from Monmouth and Ocean Counties, New Jersey." *Occasional Papers of the Museum of Zoology, University of Michigan* no. 328 (1936): 1-10.

Corn, Paul Stephen, and James C. Fogleman. "Extinction of Montane Populations of the Northern Leopard Frog *(Rana pipiens)* in Colorado." *Journal of Herpetology* 18, no. 2 (1984): 147-52.

Gosner, Kenneth L., and Irving H. Black. "The Effects of Acidity on the Development and Hatching of New Jersey Frogs." *Ecology* 38, no. 2 (1957): 256-62.

————. *"Hyla andersonii."* In *Catalog of American Amphibians and Reptiles*. American Society of Ichthyologists and Herpetologists (Nov. 1967).

————. "Larval Development of New Jersey Hylidae." *Copeia* 1 (1957): 31-36.

Johnson, Robert R. "Model Programs for Reproduction and Management: Ex Situ and In Situ Conservation of Toads of the Family Bufonidae." In *Captive Management and Conservation of Amphibians and Reptiles*, ed. James B. Murphy, Kraig Adler, and Joseph T. Collins. Ithaca, N.Y.: Society for the Study of Amphibians and Reptiles, 1994.

Means, Bruce D. "Pine Barrens Treefrog *(Hyla andersoni)*." In Florida Committee on Rare and Endangered Plants and Animals, vol. 3, *Amphibians and Reptiles* (1978): 3-4.

————, and Clive J. Longden. "Aspects of the Biology and Zoogeography of the Pine Barrens Treefrog *(Hyla andersoni)* in Northern Florida." *Herpetologica* 32, no. 2 (1976): 117-30.

Neill, Wilfred T. "Hibernation of Amphibians and Reptiles in Richmond County, Georgia." *Herpetologica* 4, no. 3 (1948): 107-14.

Noble, G. Kingsley, and Ruth C. Noble. "The Anderson Tree Frog *(Hyla andersonii* Baird), Observations on Its Habits and Life History." *Zoologica* 11, no. 18 (1923): 416-55.

Simons, Lewis. "New Jersey's Surprising Pine Barrens." *Smithsonian* 14, no. 4 (1983): 79-88.